Easy Does It!

Popular Jam Tunes You Can Play for Hammered Dulcimer

by Mark Alan Wade

Visit us on the Web at www.melbay.com — E-mail us at email@melbay.com

Dedication

To my devoted students in hopes of years of jamming to come!

Acknowledgements

I wish to thank my loving wife Cristina for
her constant love and support of my musical endeavors.

Many thanks to Dan Landrum of *Dulcimer Players* News for creative brainstorming, honest critiques, inspirational playing and treasured friendship.

Edited by master fiddler, colleague and friend,
Dr. Andrew Carlson, Denison University.

Mark's hammered dulcimers are built by:

Michael C. Allen, ~*Cloud Nine*~ Musical Instruments
17/16/8
&
Dusty Strings
D650

Contents

Foreword

We can all empathize with eager dulcimer players who are not yet able to keep up with a jam. Everyone has been there! It can be frustrating and overwhelming to try. Soon, undue embarrassment consumes them as they peck out a note or two (using their softest leather side of their hammer collection). Understandably, these capable players are often intimidated by the tricky rhythms and fast tempo of "notey" fiddle tunes (and the sheer number of them!) and sit on the sidelines of jams while more experienced players leave them in the dust. "Slow Jams" are a helpful musical outlet all of us have enjoyed at times; but often jamming on the same "notey" fiddle tunes a little slower doesn't solve the problem. After all, playing a hard song slowly does not necessarily make it easy! We simply need easier alternative versions of these tunes for those who need them while preserving the authentic versions of our rich musical heritage for those who are ready for the challenge of learning the original tunes.

The old adage, "crawl first, then walk, and then run" is great advice for learning a musical instrument. The problem in applying this advice has been that fiddle tunes and jam books only have us "run"- and running over hurdles at that. Even "running slowly" (slow jamming), is still running!

This book, *Easy Does It! Popular Jam Tunes You CAN Play*, presents these great fiddle tunes in an easy to learn, easy to play, and easy to "RUN" way for ALL ability levels. Each tune is first presented in an "Easy Does It!" version that captures all of the spirit and character of the original tune, but without all the pitfalls. These versions allow beginning and intermediate players to learn the tunes quickly and be able to keep up with a jam. I have even arranged some difficult tunes with an "Intermediate Does It!" version that bridges the gap between the easy version and the original tune when needed. These easy versions are then paired with the original tune on the adjacent page for intermediate and advanced players.

After more than 16 years of teaching these tunes, I noticed that students tend to stumble on the same things when learning new tunes. Pick-up notes in general, and those found in 1st and 2nd endings in particular, often cause students to trip rhythmically. Long streams of 8th or 16th notes often cause students to miss-hit and/or get lost. Some hazards are in the tune books themselves. Fiddle tune music is often written much too small for hammered dulcimer players to use well. Further, the music is often placed on the page with no regard for the phrase structure of the music. Fiddle tunes typically have four measure phrases that consist of a 2 bar question phrase and a 2 bar answer phrase. In this *Easy Does It!* book, all of the music is printed 40% larger than in most other jam books AND each piece is formatted so that each line begins a new musical phrase. This helps your eyes from getting lost! You will instinctively be able to tell where you are on the page when looking up from your dulcimer by what your ears naturally hear in the song's phrases- no guessing!

All of the tunes in this book have been arranged specifically for hammered dulcimer with special care given to preserve the integrity of the original tune. Even so, all of the tunes will fit on a 15/14 standard dulcimer. It is my strong personal belief that one should play with strict dominant hand lead (strong hand on strong beats) on all fiddle tunes for the strongest rhythmic drive and most intuitive hammer patterns. Certain tunes that may be less intuitive have suggested hammer patterns included for your convenience. Finally, no book can replace the need to hear fiddle tunes by expert players. After all, fiddle tunes have been passed down in an aural tradition for hundreds of years. You will enjoy your instrument and these tunes even more if you begin building a listening library of all of the great players out there.

Please enjoy these fun tunes and consider this book your license to keep up with any jam! Dulcimer clubs may purchase this book at a discounted bulk rate as a thank you for keeping our music alive! I hope to see you all at festivals or online at my website soon.

STANDARD 15/14 DULCIMER LAYOUT

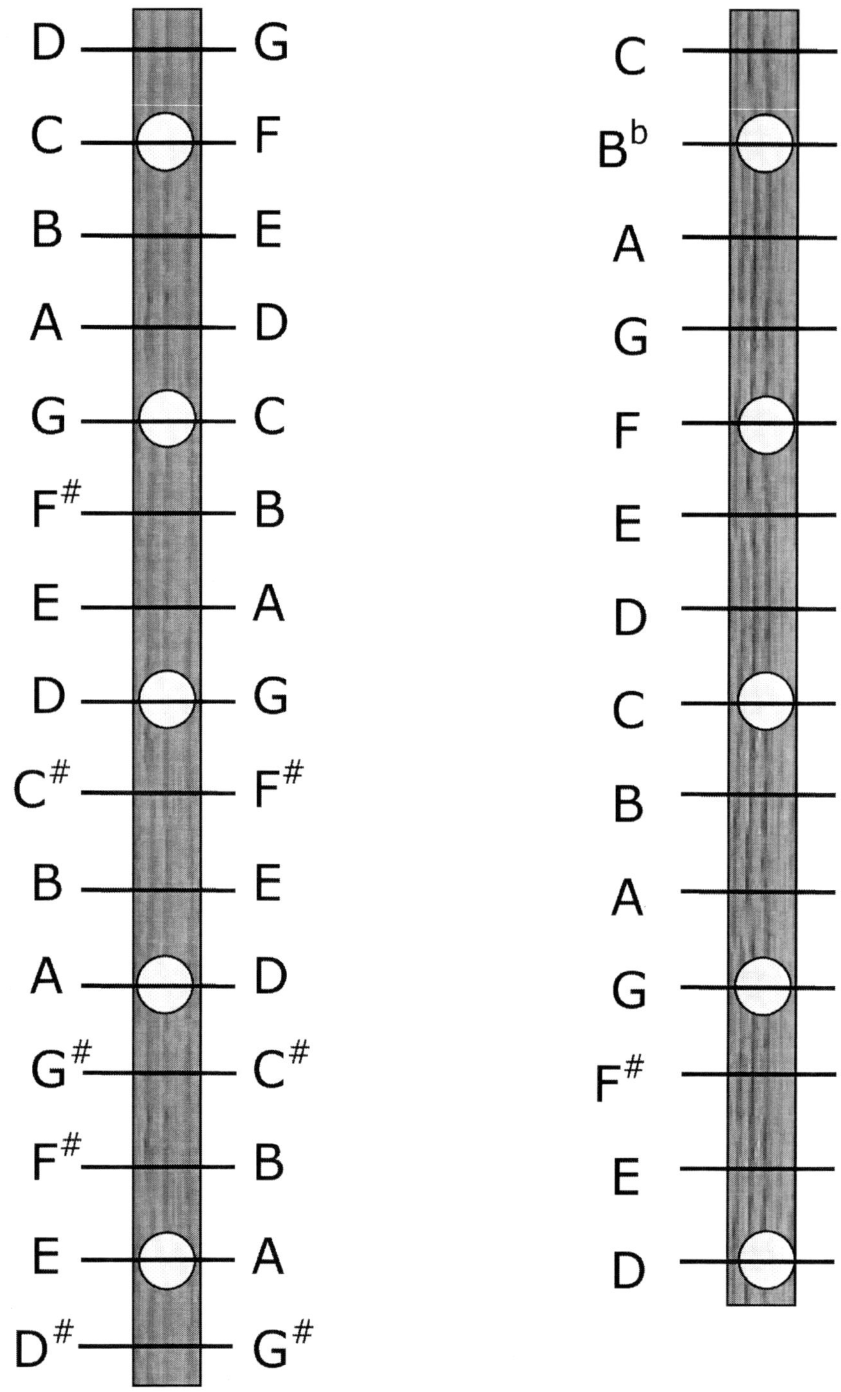

About the Author

Mark Alan Wade is an avid hammered dulcimer performer, composer and teacher. A National Hammered Dulcimer Champion, he can be heard on more than a dozen recordings and is a columnist for the *Dulcimer Players News Journal*. An active private teacher, Mark's students include the 2004 and 2007 National Hammered Dulcimer Champions.

When Mark was a student, his trumpet playing was his gateway into music schools, since the American dulcimer was not (yet) a standard conservatory instrument. His exceptional trumpeting allowed him to expand his musical limits throughout academia, which culminated in his Doctorate of Musical Arts in Trumpet Performance from The Ohio State University.All the while, the self-discipline, refinement, expressiveness, and musicality of his trumpet playing were being absorbed into his dulcimer playing. This is the very essence of Mark's unique style- a blend of traditional dulcimer playing with his formal classical training.

Currently Dr. Wade is an Assistant Professor of Music at Denison University where he teaches trumpet, music theory, and directs the wind ensemble. Mark is proud to serve the dulcimer community as the only professor in the United States offering a major in Dulcimer Performance at a NASM accredited university. In addition, Mark has toured Austria, Slovakia and Hungary as principal trumpet of the Classical Music Festival Orchestra and Brass Quintet of Eisenstadt, Austria. On various occasions, he has performed for audiences of notables including: Presidents George Bush Sr. and President Bill Clinton, Ross Perot, and the former U.S. Secretary of Defense, William S. Cohen. Wade has also performed with the Beach Boys and the Lancaster Festival Orchestra (Asst. Principal), Columbus Symphony Orchestra, West Virginia Symphony Orchestra, the Central Ohio Symphony Orchestra, Benedict College Community Orchestra (Principal), the Springfield Symphony Orchestra (Principal), and is a section member of the Newark-Granville Symphony Orchestra.

Mark and his wife, Cristina, live in New Albany, OH with their son. He has published four instructional books for hammered dulcimer as well as various arrangements of classical pieces in sheet music. More information can be found at: markalanwade.com or "friend" him on facebook.com.

John Ryan's Polka

Easy Does It!

Traditional
Arranged by Mark A. Wade

John Ryan's Polka

Traditional
Arranged by Mark A. Wade

Soldier's Joy

Easy Does It!

Traditional American
Arranged by Mark A. Wade

Soldier's Joy

Traditional American
Arranged by Mark A. Wade

Old Joe Clark

Easy Does It!

Traditional
Arranged by Mark A. Wade

Old Joe Clark

Traditional
Arranged by Mark A. Wade

June Apple

Easy Does It!

Traditional
Arranged by Mark A. Wade

June Apple

Traditional
Arranged by Mark A. Wade

Sally Goodin'

Easy Does It!

Traditional
Arranged by Mark A. Wade

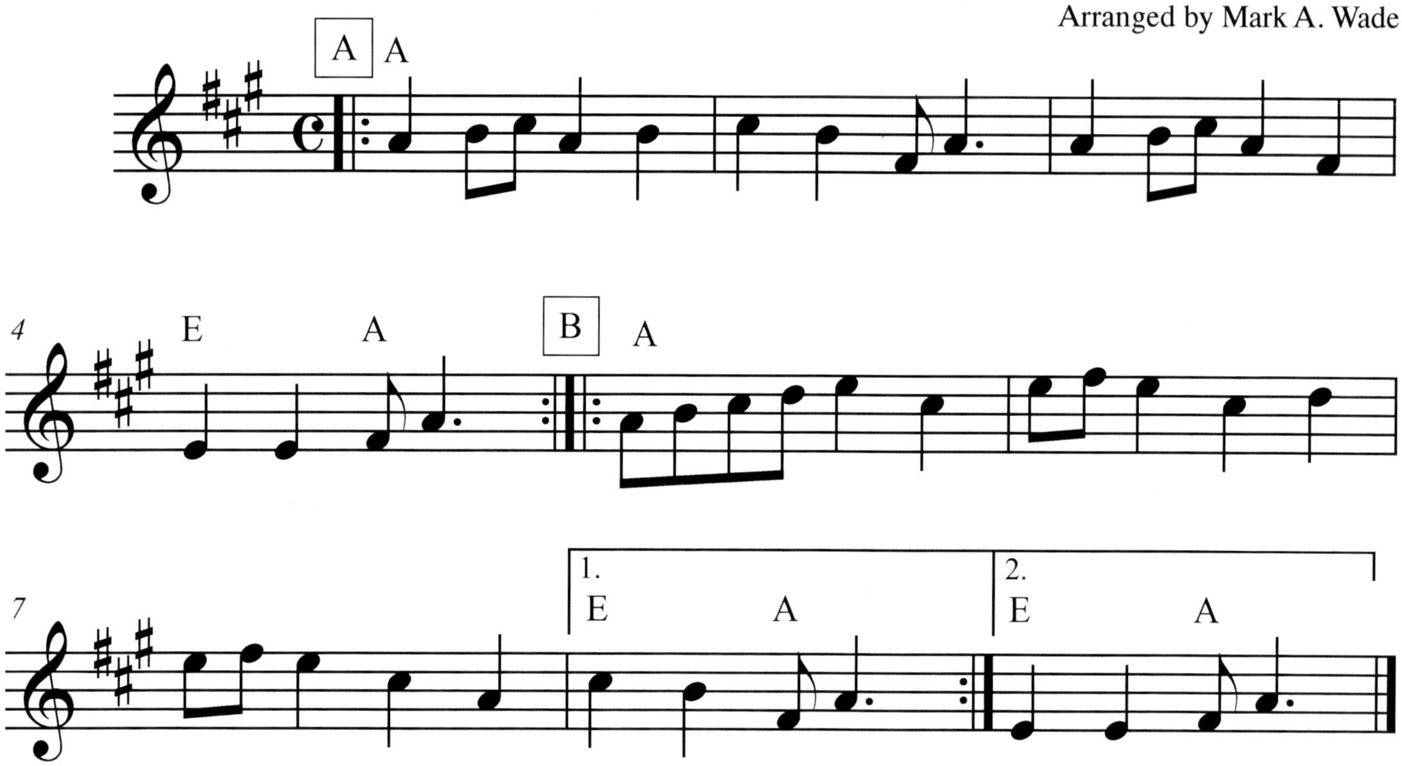

Sally Goodin'

Traditional
Arranged by Mark A. Wade

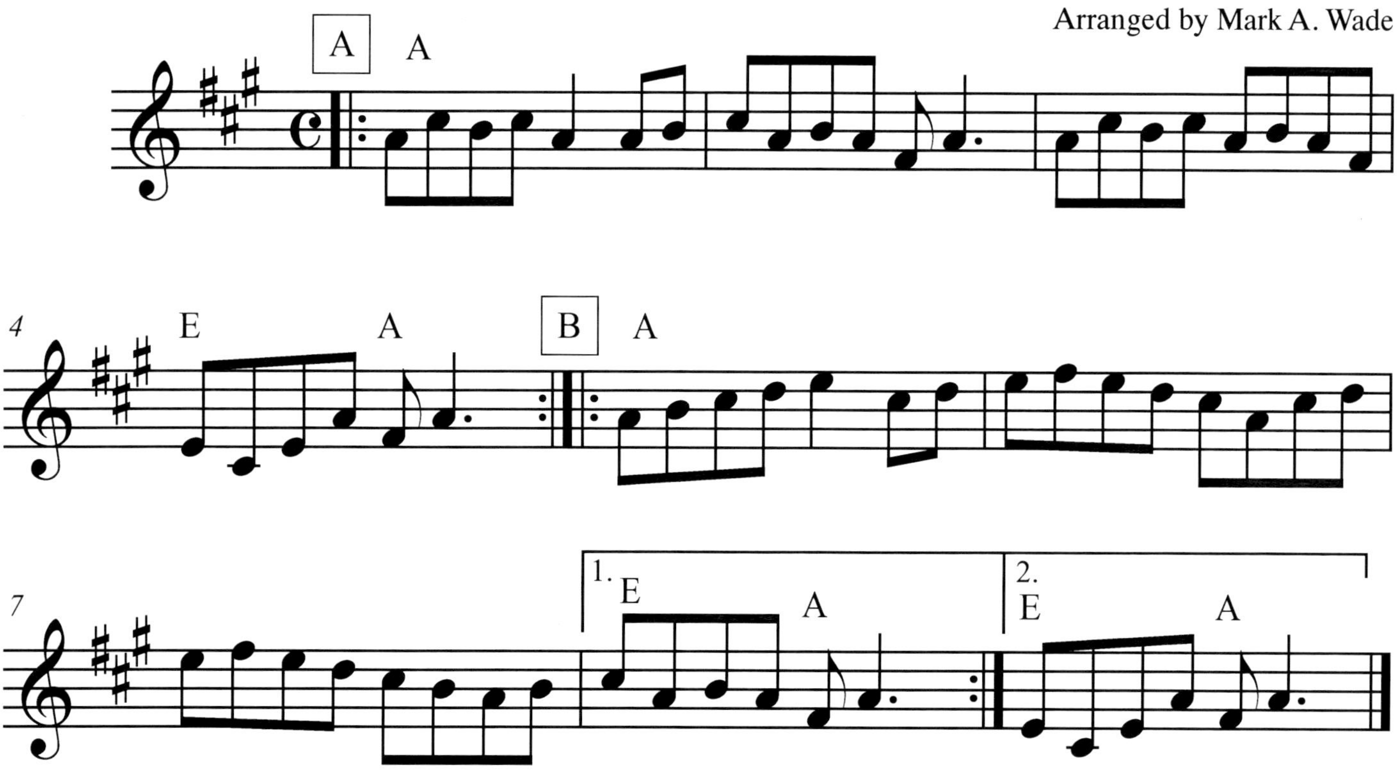

Cluck Old Hen

Easy Does It!

Traditional
Arranged by Mark A. Wade

Cluck Old Hen

Traditional
Arranged by Mark A. Wade

Saint Anne's Reel

Easy Does It!

Traditional American
Arranged by Mark A. Wade

Saint Anne's Reel

Traditional American
Arranged by Mark A. Wade

Shenandoah Falls

Easy Does It!

Traditional American
Arranged by Mark A. Wade

Shenandoah Falls

Traditional American
Arranged by Mark A. Wade

Whiskey Before Breakfast

Easy Does It!

Traditional
Arranged by Mark A. Wade

Whiskey Before Breakfast

Traditional
Arranged by Mark A. Wade

Whiskey Before Breakfast

Stylized Alternative

Traditional
Arranged by Mark A. Wade

Bonaparte's Retreat

Easy Does It!

Traditional
Arranged by Mark A. Wade

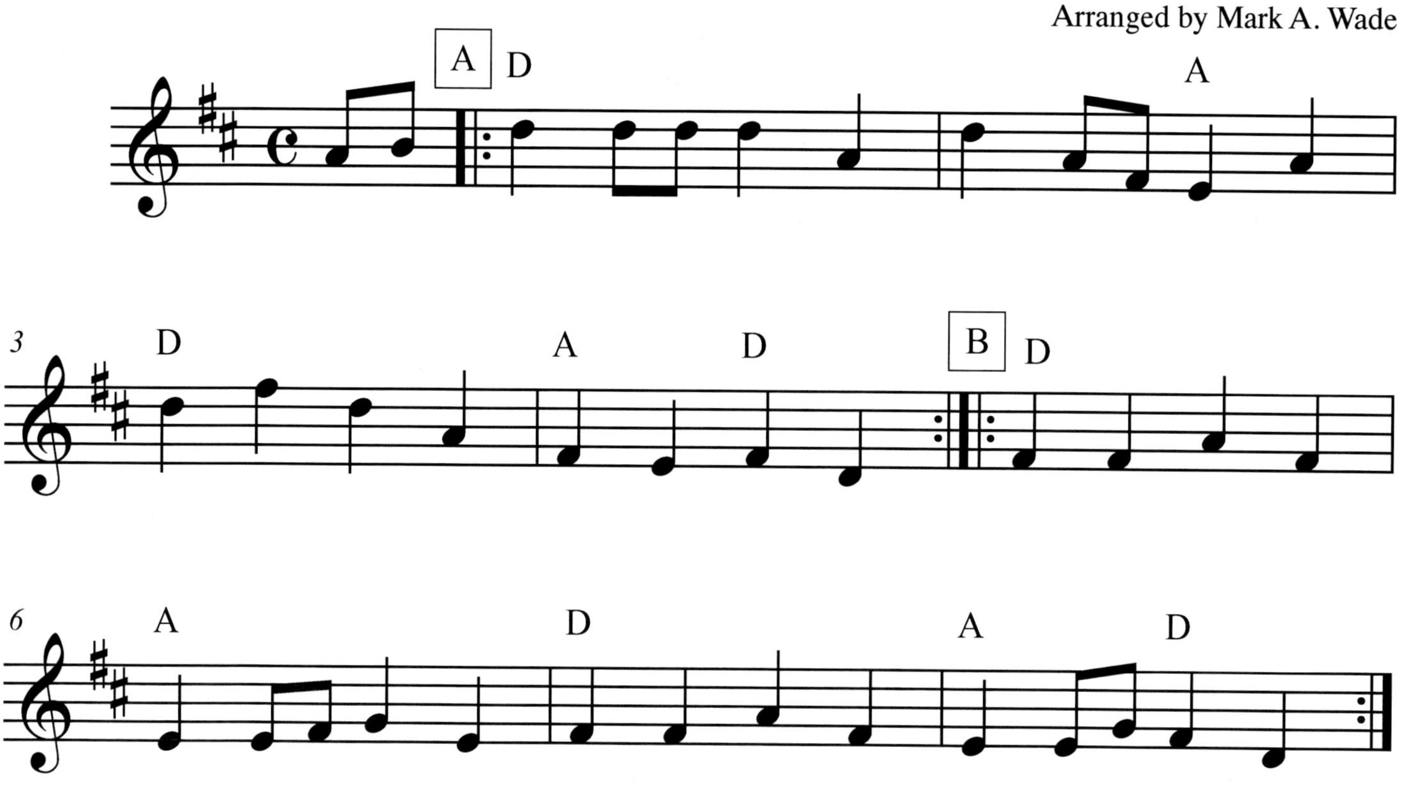

Bonaparte's Retreat

Traditional
Arranged by Mark A. Wade

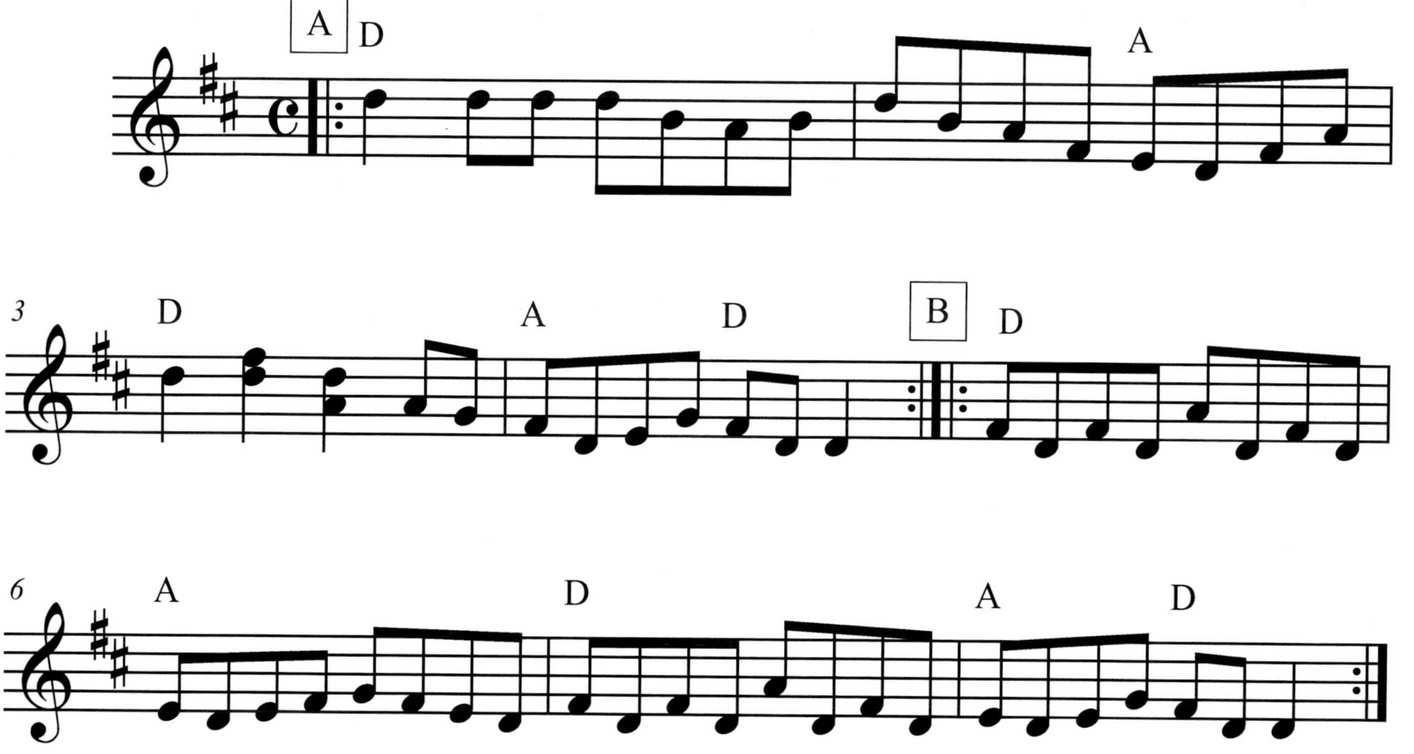

Temperance Reel

Easy Does It!

Traditional Irish
Arranged by Mark A. Wade

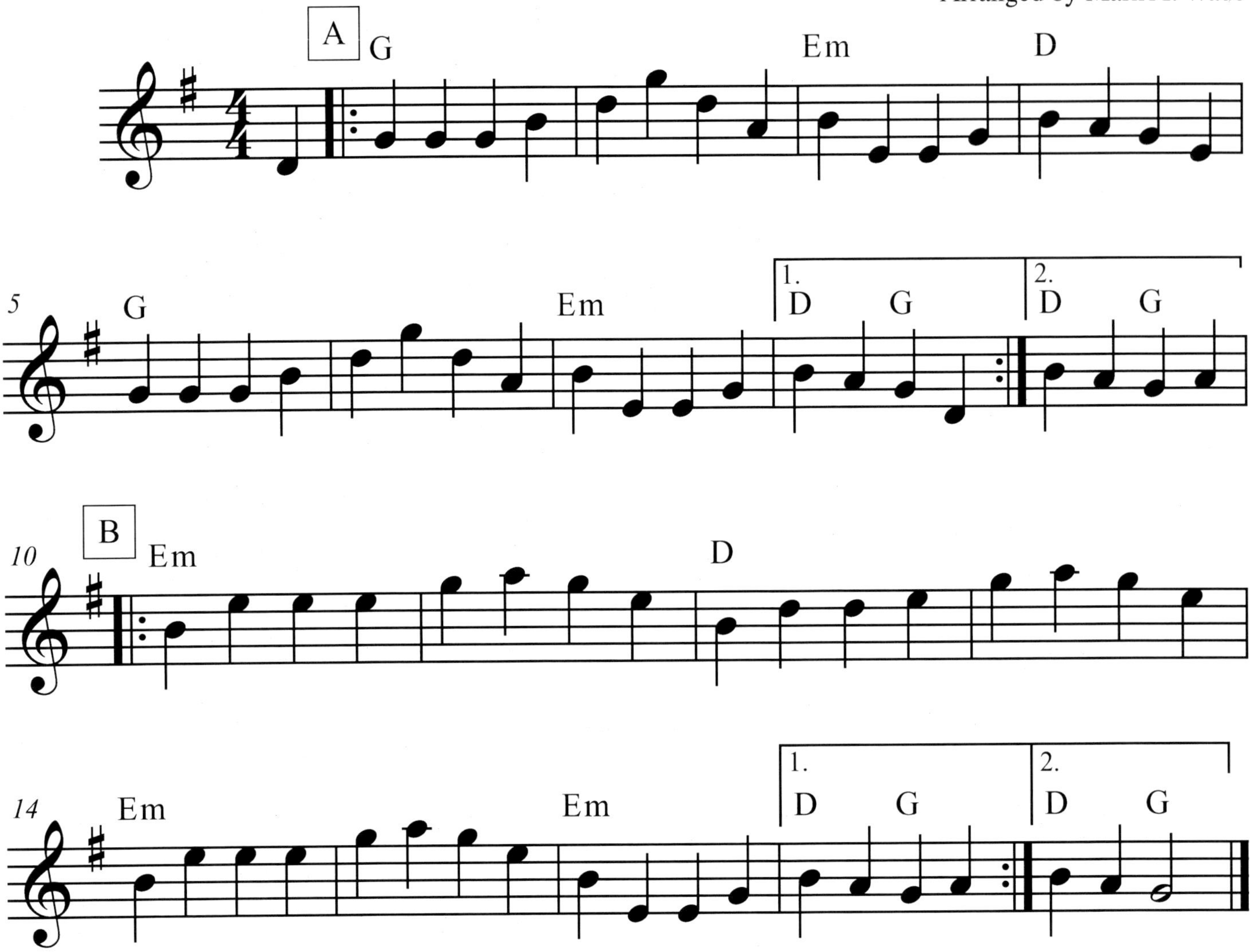

NOTE: Play this simple theme with your dominant hand ONLY.
This will teach your dominant hand where to play in the full version that follows.

Temperance Reel

Intermediate Does It!

Traditional Irish
Arranged by Mark A. Wade

N=Non-dominant Hand
D= Dominant Hand

Temperance Reel

Traditional Irish
Arranged by Mark A. Wade

N=Non-Dominant Hand
D= Dominant Hand

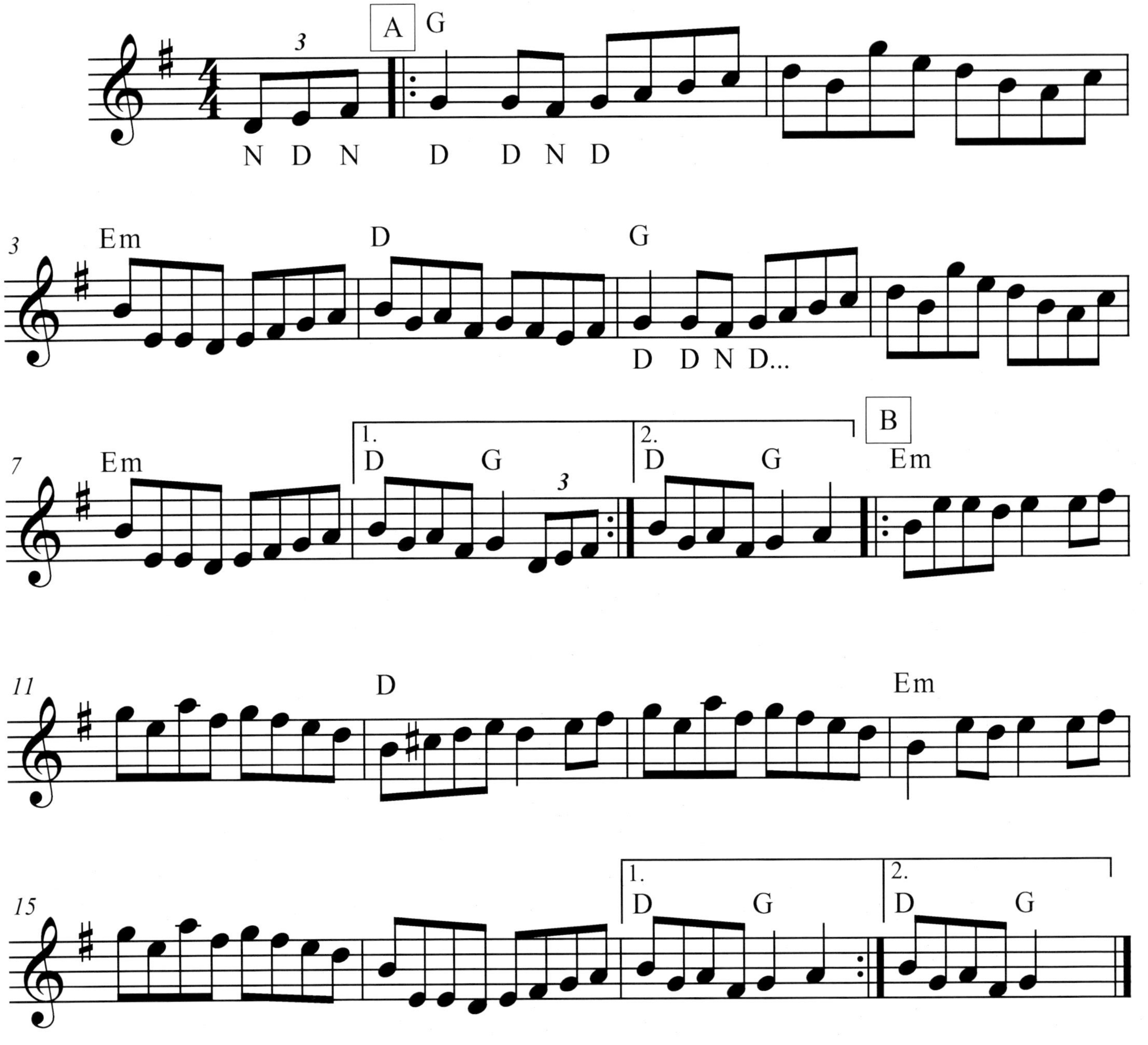

This page is intentionally left blank to avoid a page turn.

Red-Haired Boy

Easy Does It!

Traditional Irish Reel
Arranged by Mark A. Wade

Red-Haired Boy

Traditional Irish Reel
Arranged by Mark A. Wade

Stoney Point

Easy Does It!

Traditional
Arranged by Mark A. Wade

Stoney Point

Traditional
Arranged by Mark A. Wade

Cherokee Shuffle

Easy Does It!

Traditional American
Arranged by Mark A. Wade

Cherokee Shuffle

Traditional American
Arranged by Mark A. Wade

Swinging on a Gate

Easy Does It!

Traditional
Arranged by Mark A. Wade

Swinging on a Gate

Traditional
Arranged by Mark A. Wade

Sailor's Hornpipe

Easy Does It!

Traditional
Arranged by Mark A. Wade

Sailor's Hornpipe

Traditional
Arranged by Mark A. Wade

Bill Cheatham

Easy Does It!

Traditional Bluegrass
Arranged by Mark A. Wade

Bill Cheatham

Traditional Bluegrass
Arranged by Mark A. Wade

NOTES: This song is in A major and requires a high G♯ which is not on all 15/14 instruments.
*Play the alternative lower notes provided (*) if needed.
**In measures 11 and 15, play the notes with the stems up if possible.
Play the notes with stems down to avoid the us of G♯.

Drowsy Maggie

Easy Does It!

Irish Traditional
Arranged by Mark A. Wade

The aids below are for
right-handed players only.

Drowsy Maggie

Irish Traditional
Arranged by Mark A. Wade

D=Dominant hand
N = Non-Dominant Hand

NOTES: For the best rhythmic groove and the smoothest stickings, use your dominant hand for all down beats and your non-dominant hand for the off-beats. No exceptions. Trust me!

Recordings by Mark Alan Wade

Just As I Am – Mark's second album presents traditional country hymns drawn from diverse musical influences–from blues to classical. This recording features the hammered dulcimer accompanied by varied instruments, including: guitar, bass, mandolin, flute, percussion, fiddle, and vocals on three tracks. Besides *Just As I Am*, the CD includes: *Wayfaring Stranger, How Great Thou Art, Ave Maria, Simple Gifts, The Sweetest Gift* and many more. The CD was re-released in 2002 with a new track: a poignant arrangement of *The Old Rugged Cross*.

WAY Over the Waterfall – *WAY Over the Waterfall* takes traditional tunes to a new dimension of artistry with jazzy improvisations and tasty embellishments. Featured on this CD is Alex De Pue, 1999 National Fiddle Champion (Winfield, Kansas), Mark Kreis and other great musicians. This CD features great arrangements of: *Billy Bob's Blackberry Blossom Boogie (Blackberry Blossom), Lime Green Sleeves (Greensleeves), Wrongs of Man (Rights of Man), Danny Boyz (Danny Boy), Flight of the Bumble Bee-Bop* and many more.

Silver Bells – *Silver Bells*, is a delightful Christmas album filled with instrumental arrangements of holiday favorites. So original! So different! So beautiful! Mark is again accompanied by 1999 Winfield Fiddle Champ, Alex De Pue who frequents the stage of the Grand Old Opry. You will want to play this CD year-round. Includes *Silver Bells, Sleigh Ride, What Child Is This?, Canon in D, Joy to the World, O Holy Night, Winter Wonderland, Silent Night* and other Christmas favorites.

Hammer On! – Mark's ensemble project, *Hammer On!* consists of four multi-instrumentalists – all four play the guitar – all four play the hammered dulcimer – the possibilities are endless! Mark is joined by Dan Landrum, Yanni's renowned hammered dulcimer player, Randy Clepper on cittern, guitar, hammered dulcimer and tenor banjo, and Bob McMurray on guitar and hammered dulcimer. *Hammer On!* music is loaded with an arsenal of driving rhythms and hot licks. Includes: *Rondo in 7/8, Enamored, Cluck Old Hen, Falling Water, En Gedi, Sweet Georgia Brown* and others.

Serenade – Romantic classical pieces and timeless ballads on solo hammered dulcimer. Tracks include: Chopin's *Nocturne, Op.9, no.3, Clair de lune by Debussy, Prelude from Cello Suite, No.1* by J.S. Bach, *Smoke Gets In Your Eyes, The Swan* by St. Saëns, Schubert's *Ave Maria, Largo* by Rodrigo, *A Time for Us* (theme from Romeo and Juliet) and many more.